The Diary of a Preacher's Daughter:

A POETIC JOURNEY

Sheri N. Williams

❧ TABLE OF CONTENTS ❧

⋟ TABLE OF CONTENTS ⋞

Dedication

To my loving husband and my best friend: thank you for all your prayers, support, guidance and all of the work you have done to help with the release of this book!

To my family members and friends

In loving memory of my brother Willie, I know you would be proud of me.

CHAPTER ONE

THE DIARY OF A PREACHER'S DAUGHTER

I had a loving childhood and was raised by the best parents anyone could ask for. My parents have been in ministry since I was a child. There was never a dull moment growing up in a family of three brothers and two sisters. We all were loved and well cared for. We were "fixtures" in our father's church. We grew up serving in the ministry with the same love and passion our parents had for the ministry. We lived and breathed ministry.

People often hold pastors' children to higher standards than other children. If someone else's child gets kicked out of school, it's bad; but if a preacher's kid, best known as a "PK," gets kicked out of school, it's "baaaad!" People often say, "PK's are bad." Personally, I never understood how a child, doing the same thing as another child, would be considered bad because he or she was a PK. There was a lot of pressure growing up as a pastor's child. I had that feeling that everyone was watching and waiting on me to fall so they could say, "and your daddy is the preacher."

In the third grade, I was teased and fought as a result of being bullied. After winning my first fight, I vowed to never allow anyone to pick on me again. I continued fighting into middle school, even started bullying and picking on other students. I was sent home frequently from school for fighting.

It was only a matter of time before I received my wakeup call. At age 14, I was involved in a fight that progressed over three days. The fight ended with me being hit in the head with a horseshoe stake and almost losing my life. Although I had a couple of fights after that incident, I eventually stopped fighting and became a motivational speaker advocating nonviolence and encouraging youth to walk away from violence. My parents prayed fervently for me and I'm thankful for them. I thank God I made it through that period in my life.

At age 18, I experienced another huge pitfall which took me on a silent, emotional rollercoaster. Only God knew my struggles and pain. I started writing and these writings served as an outlet through that season of my life. These poems and poetic prayers were written during a three-year period. I held onto them for over 10 years, and now I present these raw writings, unaltered and unchanged. These writings carried me through the tough periods of my life. I wrote them to God since I felt like I couldn't share my feelings with family, close friends or church members. I was a PK and people often placed PKs on a pedestal. It was almost like since my father was the pastor, I was supposed to be perfect and the moment I made a mistake it would be magnified. So what I am sharing with you has been shared with only a few.

People often dissect other people's lives with the tendency to forget that they are also human and prone to making mistakes. Maybe some people haven't read the scripture that says, "All have sinned and come short of the glory of God." Some forget that PKs are bound to make mistakes, fight temptations and have to work out their own salvation, just like everyone else. Perhaps it makes some people feel good to know that the pastor's kids are not perfect, but newsflash: we never said we were perfect. Please kindly take all PKs off the pedestal and allow them the same grace, mercy and love of God available to all believers. Remember, we are all running this race and walking this walk daily. At times we may get detoured. We may become tired, and even fall. The good news is that as long as we get back up and keep moving, we will make it.

Many may be surprised at what they'll read going forward, but that's ok. This book will show how PKs too are human and encounter troubles like every other person. They should never be placed on a pedestal. If they do fall, know they can get back up. Though I reflect upon my experiences through the eyes of a PK, allow me to encourage anyone who has ever sinned and fallen short by saying that no matter what people may think or say, God loves you. God will deliver you, set you free, and can use your misery as a testimony to minister to someone else. This book is designed to enlighten, encourage and enable each of you to walk into the liberty of God, free from condemnation.

So follow me on this poetic journey as I share from *The Diary of a Preacher's Daughter*. Word of warning: this journey is not for the faint-hearted, the self-righteous or the judgmental. It is for those who are seeking grace, redemption and restoration.

CHAPTER TWO

DEAR LORD...

"I cried unto the LORD with my voice; with my voice unto the LORD did I make my supplication."
Psalm 142:1

Dear Lord,

You know who this is; I finally got the guts,
I was afraid to come to You because I kept messing up.
It seems the more I try to change, the harder it gets;
All these trials the enemy set up are making me sick.
You brought me out of darkness and into Your marvelous light,
Yet I left and returned to the same mess, what an ugly sight!
Lord, I need strength-mad strength, to resist the enemy,
I'm talking about being prayed and fasted up, reading my word because
You know my flesh is killing me.
Lord, I was on the right path, but I took a wrong turn,
The devil tried to trip me up so in the end I would burn.
But I told the devil, "You better get under my feet!"
I saw right through his tricks and I wasn't about to keep getting beat.
So I prayed and I fasted and I read Your word,
So that when the enemy came I would be ready and I wasn't "scurred."
Now I'm doing alright Lord, I know who I am in You,
That old man is in the past because Your word says,
"All things are made new."
I just want to thank You for forgiving me of my sins,
I know that You are there and will be until the end.

Love Your daughter,
Sheri

Dear Lord,

It seems I'm at a down point in my life,
Everything's going wrong, nothing is going right.
I've been used and taken advantage of,
It seems everybody's got a scam and wants to rip me off.
I can't get it right no matter how hard I try,
It seems my life is falling apart and I don't know why.
I've been drifting through life for quite a while,
Now it seems where the wind takes me, I just go and smile.
But I'm not happy about the state I'm in;
I wonder, am I reaping or suffering from my past sin?
It seems I'm in a circle and I can't get out,
No matter how hard I try, scream and shout.
I know I can't change, doing it on my own,
So Jesus I need You, please won't you help me out.
I'm sorry for my sins and everything I've done, Lord,
I need You to make it better and save me from this cruel
world.
I promise I won't put anything before You again,
I promise I'll let You lead; I'll follow you 'til the end.

Love Your daughter,
Sheri

Dear Lord,

It seems the more I try to do right, I keep doing wrong.
Lord, I love You and I need You; please take me back in
Your arms.
This walk is not easy; You never said it was,
I struggle every day to please You, but it seems like I keep
falling short.
I need strength to help me resist the things of this world,
Lord, I need You as a covering to protect me, this young,
Christian girl.
Lord, my flesh is a mess; please help me decrease it;
Strengthen and feed my spirit man.

Love Your daughter,
Sheri

Dear Lord,

I know right from wrong,
Yet, my flesh tries to make me push wisdom under the rug.
But it's not going to happen,
My sins are about to go out with the bath water in the tub.
I'm tired of giving in to the flesh, then later, I'm feeling bad,
It's time to loose my spirit man and be free to run rampant.
I don't care and won't care about the things of this world
anymore,
All of these things are temporary and can't compare to the
things my Father has in store.

Love Your daughter,
Sheri

Dear Lord,

I am on a mission, for I know I will not be here forever,
I can't get cozy or snug;
It's time for me to speak my spiritual mind and stop pushing
it under the rug.
Lord, help me as I take a stand to be a mighty soldier in Your
army.
We both know the enemy is thinking of a plan to trip me up,
Lord, prepare me ahead of time so I will know when he is
going to strike.

Love Your daughter,
Sheri

Dear Lord,

I love You, You're my everything!
My icing on the cake,
My cover that keeps me warm,
You're my father and my friend, on You I can depend.
Please forgive me for my sins,
For I know I am not worthy of Your blessings or Your ear,
But if You could just forgive me of my sins, I would be so happy.
I just want to feel Your presence, to know that You still care,
To know that You still love me, and will always be there.
Oh God, I can barely speak because I don't feel worthy enough for You to listen to me,
I thought I'd just write it down so You could look and see.
I had to get it out some way, but I felt too condemned to pray,
Lord, I want to be strong for You, please guide me and show me the way,
Because I don't want to be led astray.
I need You as my guide; oh let me not be confused, tossed to and fro,
Let me know what Your will is.
And what way I shall go Lord, oh merciful You are,
I just want to be more like You, and like You I will be.

Love Your daughter,
Sheri

Dear Lord,

I don't know what to say, I'm crying all the time,
I cannot stand my flesh; I want Your will, not mine.
I find myself looking at others' short comings,
And forgetting about my downfalls and the grace and mercy
You showed me.
I am far from perfect, but I'm trying to reach the mark,
I'm trying to fight my fleshly man so I may have a holy walk.
I'm fighting Lord, I'm fighting; I want to please You so,
I love Your holy spirit,
I love Your holy ghost,
Please forgive me for my sins, that I will not repeat it.
Again, help me to stay humble before You,
And to my enemies be a friend.
More of You and less of me is my prayer today,
More of You and less of me is what I must continue to say.
I love You, Jesus.

Love Your daughter,
Sheri

Dear Lord,

Lord, please hold me; I don't know what to do,
I'm lonely, I'm hurting, I'm really going through.
No one to talk to, all I want is You!
To rock me and hold me and tell me what to do,
Can't stop crying, I'm trying but the wounds are too deep,
Please bandage my wounds, please come and save me.
Can't breathe, can't think, I'm hurting too bad,
There's a war going on inside me and it's got me really bad.
Please, oh God hear me; hear my heart as it beats,
I'm lonely, please hold me, I'm wounded and weak.
I just need Your love, Your arms,
Stretched out wide,
Protect me, correct me, help my fleshly man die.
I need You! I'm confused, many things on my mind,
And nobody hears me, no one pays me any mind,
Except You Lord, my savior.
You care how I feel,
You know I am trying so hard to do Your will.
Please send forth Your strength to help me be strong,
Please send forth Your blood to wash away all the wrong
I'm nothing without You; I know that, I do,
I'm glad to have a best friend, a best friend like You.
I love You, Lord.
P.S. Please forgive me.

Love Your daughter,
Sheri

CHAPTER THREE

CONVERSATIONS WITH THE LORD

"Behold, the LORD'S hand is not shortened, that it cannot save; neither his ear heavy, that it cannot hear:"
Isaiah 59:1

I'm Sorry / Forgive Me

Jesus I'm sorry, I'm sorry.

I'm sorry for taking Your love for granted and sinning behind

Your back,

I'm sorry for failing the test, and allowing my spirit man to

get off track.

I'm sorry if I ever compromised to please man or myself,

I'm sorry for not coming to You first, all the times I needed

help.

I'm sorry for going back on my word and committing that

same sin,

I'm sorry for running to others for encouragement, and

coming to You in the end.

I'm sorry for being mean and nasty to my enemies, family

members and friends,

I'm sorry for everything I've done that I didn't realize was a

sin.

Please forgive me, Lord,

I'll try harder because I really want to please You, Lord,

Please forgive me for not reading my word and having a dull

two-edged sword.

I know You expect more from me,

And I am accounted for what I know.

Please wash me with Your precious blood,

And make me white as snow.

It's Not Just People

Lord, why do people hurt me so?

Am I reaping the seeds that I once sowed?

Or is this a test, or maybe a trial?

I know I'm not perfect, I'm not in denial.

But so-called friends lie and talk about me behind my back,

Loved ones who I need the most are always on my attack.

It seems today that love has waxed cold and it's all about

hate,

Oh Lord, when is it going to stop? Oh soon I pray.

No one listens; they just want people to hear them talk,

Everybody's right, nobody's wrong, and if You don't like it

take a walk.

Reality is there is a real devil out there seeking whom he may

devour,

People are just being used by him and the demons he hired.

So it's not people, my friends and family,

But it's the enemy who uses them to try to get to me.

Thank You Lord for the understanding,

And helping me not to react by having hate in my heart.

I almost wanted to become a mean person, but You stopped it

before it could start.

If You are my savior and had to go through, too,

You fed and healed people, and ministered to them, too.

Yet Your disciple whom You loved betrayed You,

Thank You for opening up my blind eyes to see,

It's not always people; sometimes they are being used by the

enemy.

Your Love Is Swell

Lord, I fought people for no reason,

Yet, You still love me.

I did things against Your will and You

Showed me mercy,

I sinned over and over again, and fornicated too.

When I looked up, who was on my side?

Nobody but you.

You turned me around and took me

Out of the miry clay,

You made me humble, imparted in me love

And a willing mind to pray.

Lord, if You did it for me, I know You can do it for that

murderer, too,

And for the liars, cheaters, homosexuals and adulterers

You'll also make new.

And for the thieves and drug dealers who You love so dear as

well

You know what God, I want You to know

I think Your love is swell.

Screaming Lord Help Me

I'm pregnant,

So many emotions,

What am I going to do?

Tears run down my face,

Drops on my shoes,

In shock, I'm 18, what to do?

What will people say?

And how will they treat me?

This has ruined everything.

I think I'll drive somewhere far away,

So I won't have to deal with all the judgmental faces.

I already know people are waiting for me to fail,

So they can talk about me being a PK, unwed and pregnant

Wait, I just need to exhale.

Lord why me, why now? I don't know what to do,

Feeling like ending my life would be better than sharing this

news.

A punch in my stomach, that will do the trick!

Get it together, Sheri; these thoughts are getting sick,

Ok, take a deep breath; now let it out,

I guess it's not so bad; I just have to figure this out.

I'll have to get a job and work hard for this baby,

I'll figure it out, although the situation is crazy.

I'm going to be a mother; wow, I'm going to have a baby,

I still can't share this with anyone yet, I'm scared; I'm a PK

and the pressure is heavy.

You can't keep this baby, do you know what it will do?

It will make your parents look bad; people will talk about

them and you.

What kind of life will you have? And you can forget about

school,

This baby is not happening, there's no going back.

What was I thinking? I'm confused and hopeless,

This is tearing me apart, does anyone notice?

This choice is bigger, bigger than me,

I can't deal with this pressure, I can't make them a mockery.

The people at church, they can't find out,

So I'll keep this to myself and hope I don't drown.

In the corner I sit, lost and hopeless,

Apart of me ripped out without a chance.

I wish I was stronger and faced the storm,

But I wasn't strong enough and now my baby is gone.

If you're a PK, a saint or an unbeliever too,

I shared this experience just for you.

I plead with you to not take this route,

Don't abort your child, let God work it out.

If you're not ready to be a mother, then keep the store closed,

If you find yourself with child, please let it grow.

It's not the child's fault that you were caught in sin,

And murder is not the way to handle fornication!

Don't worry about those who talk about you,

Many of them were or are in sin, too.

It's just they didn't get caught, or maybe were on birth

control,

Don't feed into their remarks, but into God's arms, go.

He will love you in spite of all that you do,

He will rock you in His arms and comfort you, too.

Don't get me wrong, don't run to sin; but if you slip up, know

Jesus is still your friend,

On Him you can depend, He will forgive all of your sins.

I wish I ran to Him sooner, but I can't go back,

Moving forward I know that He is always there,

It is Him who brought me through the times I wanted to give

up without a care.

You see the shame and the guilt was eating me up,

Crying late at night tears to fill up a

Cup

Cup

Cup

CHAPTER FOUR

POETIC FLOW

I'm Tired

I'm tired of sinning

I'm tired of people talking about me behind my back, then in

my face grinning

I'm tired of crying

I'm tired of people acting like they're for me, lying

I'm tired of all these kids out here dying

I'm tired of backsliding

I'm tired of sinners sweeping their dirt underneath the rug,

thinking they're hiding

I'm tired of setbacks

I'm tired of the enemy who's always on attack

I'm tired of giving

I'm tired of trying to walk straight and always tripping

I'm tired of people

I'm tired of fakeness and all things unreal

I'm tired of hatred

I'm tired of people passing

Secrets that are supposed to be sacred

I'm tired of jealousy

I'm tired of people hating on the gifts that God gave me

I'm tired! Lord, I'm tired

Only thing I can do is lift Your name up higher

But I still have hope in You

Because through all of this, You brought me through.

Smiling Faces Tell Lies

Some people say smiling faces tell lies,

That means I could be smiling but my soul is crying.

If I said that wasn't true, then I would be lying; there is no

denying

There's a smile on my face, but my soul is dying.

My feelings were hurt and I felt really bad

But I laughed it off so I wouldn't look bad.

This grin on my face may look like it is shaking,

Cause I'm hurting inside and this grin I'm just faking.

I cried all night long but you wouldn't know,

Not the way I was smiling when I walked in the door.

In some ways that isn't always true,

Sometimes I can laugh and smile 'til I'm blue.

Sometimes I'm so happy I can't help but to smile,

The joy I feel inside seems to last for a while.

Sometimes I will smile and I don't even try,

And I'm filled with happiness not knowing why.

So, you see that saying is not always true,

All smiling faces aren't lying to you.

Sometimes they're sincere and yes, the smile is real,

So cheer up and smile, even if you're hurting still.

Questions

Sometimes I think, what should I do?

So many trials and tribulations I'm going through,

Sometimes I think, what should I say?

My thoughts I can't express, all I can do is pray,

Sometimes I think, I am doing something wrong.

Am I fulfilling the purpose God had for me all along?

But then I think to myself and say,

You just need to stop thinking so much, and go somewhere

and pray.

So on my knees I go to God,

Asking for guidance and wisdom out loud.

Can You hear me, oh God?

Can You see my tears?

Can You feel my pain?

Do You know my fears?

He answers, "Yes, I know all you see,

And not even you know yourself like me."

I nod and smile, yes God, You're right,

This is Your perfect will, to get to the next level I must fight.

I just needed strength and assurance from You,

Because without You, I would not know what to do.

You give me comfort, You give me peace,

In You, oh God, I get my release.

I am free from pain and worry and fear,

Because I know You, oh God, are standing near.

Every time I feel too tired to press

I'll get down on my knees, pray

And let You do the rest.

A Story

There is a story behind every face

Of the child you see grinning everyday

Some hurt and sadness

Some pain, some fear

Waiting for someone with an open ear

To listen, to care, to send up a prayer

To help, to heal, to trust, to be real

Jesus is the one who can fulfill their needs

Who comforts them at times they cannot sleep

When they call His name, He hears their call

He picks them up every time they fall

He protects and shields when danger is near

He gives them courage and takes away their fear

There is a story behind the face

Of the child you see grinning everyday

Though storms come their way

You can never tell

Because Jesus calmed the storm

And His love is swell.

What is Your Destination?

This is the preparation for your destination,

Will you choose salvation or this worldly nation?

Look back to creation, God sent His Word,

Which is the information and education of God's will for this

generation.

Yet we seem to have set His word aside to take a vacation,

Causing a separation between us and Him, ruining the

invitation of everlasting life,

Making a reservation for misery and strife.

Make an observation what is your location,

Are you on the devil's plantation?

Receiving torturous acts of radiation with feelings and

thoughts of desperation?

Or are you receiving an imputation from Jesus Christ?

Who died that we might have everlasting life and become a

holy nation,

And choose salvation,

So that we may reign with Him in the heavenly nation.

What is your destination?

Stone Cold Reality

So many people confused about religion

Others don't care, they're just stuck in tradition

God's word is the truth, don't you ever forget

If your faith is in a man or woman, you better repent

Some of us are just practicing our parent's religion

Others are believing anything just to keep the relationship

they're in.

Some of us say we are God's children

And we don't even know who He is

We won't even open up the Bible to read about Him, but we

claim we are His

It's time for us to open our eyes to the realness of God

But the reality is, we're so easily moved by the tricks of the

enemy, which is a facade

That we turn our eyes and believe everything else in the

world

Except God.

No Voice

Have you ever felt like you had no voice?

Many thoughts and ideas but had no choice.

Your inside is screaming out, what about this?

But every comment you make is shut down and thrown in the

garbage.

It's like, your candle was lit and someone blew it out.

It's like, you could feel the rain and opened your eyes to a

drought.

It's like, the greatest joy you've ever felt,

And then a punch in the face.

It's like, being ahead of all of the runners and being yanked

To the end of the race.

It's like a sunny day ruined by a storm,

It's like, a beautiful statue that suddenly lost its form.

Have you ever felt like you had no voice?

Many thoughts and ideas but had no choice.

It's like beautiful fireworks turned into dust,

A beautiful car covered with rust.

I've felt this way many times in my life,

I've learned in this walk, it's not about me,

It's about the people in this world that need to be free.

Free from the world and made new in Christ,

To be rescued from darkness and brought into light.

To know that God sent Jesus to die for our sins,

And that on the third day He rose again.

It's about helping people to know that salvation is key,

To deliverance, peace and all the heavenly things.

So yes, I've felt like I had no voice,

Many ideas and thoughts, but had no choice.

But then I remembered, it's not about me,

It's about Jesus Christ, and all the hope He brings.

I am no longer my own, for I am bought with a price,

My purpose is to serve God and lead others to Christ.

That voice I spoke of was my flesh you see,

Which has to decrease daily so my spirit can supersede.

God's will is perfect, He always has the final say,

So I have to line up with His word and before Him lay,

My voice is no longer mine, but on behalf of the greater One

I must speak,

I must allow Him to use me and my fleshly man decrease.

Have you ever felt like you had no voice?

Many thoughts and ideas but had no choice?

This Is Not My Home

Misery and strife is what I see going on in this life

People struggling, trying to make a dollar

Guys cursing a girl out cause she don't want to "holla"

People on the street doing anything to survive

Christians, stuck in tradition, always trying to compromise

Wives cheating on their husbands

Men cheating on their wives,

People trying to catch a thrill, catch a case, getting high.

Men sleeping with men and women doing the same

People rapping about sex, drugs and money and putting the

thanks in God's name.

Everybody wants to be seen on the big screen

It's all about money, status and oh yes, the "bling, bling!"

Marijuana smoking, cigarette choking, enticing beer

commercials

Children of God clubbing all night, showing up late for choir

rehearsal

Kids killing kids at the drop of a dime

They'll be lucky if they make it through high school without

dying.

Well I've made up in my mind that this life is not for me

I will not sell my soul to the devil for fame, sex, drugs or

money

I will not give in to the enemy who only comes to kill, steal

and destroy

I will not fall for the devil's decoy.

My Father in heaven has prepared a place for me

That is far more loving and beautiful than this world could

ever be

This world down here cannot begin to compare,

As for this world I am just visiting here

This is not my home.

This World

This world is cruel

Cruel indeed,

Due to the lack of love

In which we need.

This world is lost

With blinded eyes,

While the enemies lurking

In his disguise.

Though he's right in our face

We cannot see,

For we are blinded by lust

Pride and material things.

So we tend to fight against one another

Not knowing it's the enemy and not

Our sister or brother.

We're caught up in the fad

And the world's popularity

Compromising for all of these worldly things.

Jesus Christ is here for the taking,

But we accept the world

And God we're forsaking.

The times are changing and judgment is near,

It's sad that some will wait too long to hear.

This world is cruel

Cruel indeed,

Due to the lack of love

In which we all need.

The Life of a Saint

The life of a saint, now that ain't easy,

You're going to go through sometimes; life ain't always

going to be breezy

You'll learn this walk is not about feelings and me, me, me

But you'll learn to be humble and call on G-O-D.

Sometimes you'll even have to give up your right to be right,

Sometimes you'll have to starve your flesh just to win the

fight.

The life of a saint, now that ain't easy,

You're going to go through sometimes; life ain't always

going to be breezy

Some people will persecute you when you have done

something wrong,

And many places you go you'll find out, you don't belong.

And when that feeling comes you should rejoice,

Because God loves to hear a peculiar person's voice.

The life of a saint, now that ain't easy,

You're going to go through sometimes; life ain't always going to be breezy.

I'm More Than Just a Pretty Face

I'm more than just a pretty face

Stop looking at my features, go deep inside

See where my goals and ambitions hide

I hurt like you, I feel I do

I worry and yes, sometimes I cry

You think I have it easy

I say I don't

I have to deal with creeps who don't understand, "No!"

Who want to take advantage of pretty little me

Who don't care about what's inside and don't want to see

I'm more than just a pretty face, can't you see

There's a soul, a beautiful soul deep down inside of me

Most often sought after to make a man look good

In turn, I hurt inside because I am misunderstood

Why can't I be nice, why do I have to be stuck up

And ladies because of my looks you want to fight me, for

what?

But wait let me remember, where much is given much is

required

So all those regrets I now retire

For it is God who made us for purpose you see

And maybe mines is to let you know the real meaning of

beauty.

Beauty starts from within and not outside,

Often times outside is where ugliness hides.

We need to look deeper than a face, deeper than the skin,

Because the bottom line is beauty starts from within.

If My Mind Could Speak

If my mind could speak

You might not like me

You might find out a lot about me

Though I smile, you'll find out

I don't always agree

You'll see the good things hidden inside me

If my mind could speak

You might get offended

You might find out

I don't like the way myself

And you are sinning

If my mind could speak

You'll see my first love and find out

It's not you, but really the Lord God above

If my mind could speak

You probably would see

That every time my flesh

Gives in it really hurts me

When you make jokes, I laugh it off

But it really makes me sad

When you yell at me in my face

It makes me feel real bad

If my mind could speak

You would see that I have everlasting joy no matter how

Badly treated I've been

Because I know that one day

Jesus is taking me with Him to heaven

You

You saved me

Forgave me

I praise thee

For everything

You washed me

And cleansed me

Made new me

Restored me

I thank thee

For everything

You covered me

Protected me

Forgave me

You led me

You fed me

You gave me

You saved me

I thank thee

You chose me

I know thee

You woke me

I heard thee

You spoke to me

You healed me

You saved me

Forgave me

You chose me

I know thee

I thank thee

I love thee

Jesus

Men Pleasers

Men pleasers, that's what we have become

Looking for praises of men instead of God's Son

Compromising that has become our addiction

Leaving God, our first love, to join Satan's religion

Idolizing that's what we indulge in

Worshipping man as a god which is a great sin

Stench in God's nostrils, that's what we have become

Trying to serve two masters which cannot be done

Hypocrites that's how we are seen

Preaching to others, but doing the opposite things

Sell outs that's where we are now

Sold our soul for fame, fortune and a house

Please believe in the end you will be miserable

I hope you find that your eternity is livable

Men pleasers.

Hell

Lord, going to hell, I think that's crazy

I wouldn't take a peek if someone paid me

Lord why do we play with Your grace as if we have forever

If we think we have forever

We must not be very clever

But we love to get our party on and drink our booze

But we don't realize reality until it's too late

Then we lose

We lose our chance to make it into heaven and see Your face

We lose our chance because we gave up and are too lazy to

finish the race

Now instead of being on the right side we're on the left

It's sad if we don't realize our mistakes until judgment day,

Until our death.

Lover of My Soul

Holy redeemer

Lover of my soul

Heavenly Host

Lover of my soul

King of Glory

Lover of my soul

Comforter and safety

Lover of my soul

Mighty way maker

Lover of my soul

Prince of peace

Lover of my soul

My provider

Lover of my soul

My protector

Lover of my soul

My strong tower

Lover of my soul

You are my peace

Lover of my soul

Secret Place

When nothing is going right and everything seems wrong

Go to that place, you know the one;

When your body is tired and your spirit man is weak.

Go to that place where you go when you can't sleep.

When the enemy is attacking and you don't know what to do,

Run to the place where you got all your breakthroughs.

When everyone's against you

And you have no friends,

Go to that place and call on the one you can depend.

When the doctors give up and say there's nothing they can

do,

Rush to that place where your strength gets renewed.

The secret place, you know the one

Where you told God all your secrets and all your problems,

Where you worshipped the Lord

In spirit and in truth,

Where you kneeled down on your knees

And prayed when there was nothing you could do,

Where you asked for forgiveness for all the wrong you have

done

Go to your secret place and when you leave,

You'll know that Jesus has already worked out

Everything.

Everything

I know that it was God who got me through and Jesus was

my best friend who I could run to,

talk to and share,

In spite of how much I beat myself up, He always cares,

He loves me, forgave me, restored me and more

Everything I am I owe to the Lord

It was 2009 when God totally delivered me

I was instantly freed, guilt and shame had to leave

This was the year my husband and I started our ministry

And one Sunday he asked me to preach

I spoke about worship and praise, you see

But in the midst of that message, God delivered me.

I didn't plan on sharing my story; no, it wasn't in my notes

But somehow I did and even as I spoke, I felt the Holy Spirit

free me from years of hurt.

I realized God forgave me years ago, but it was me who was

doing the beating

Constantly remembering my past sins and feeling unworthy

His word says "There is therefore now no condemnation to

those who are in Christ Jesus, who walk not after the flesh

but after the spirit."

So God was no longer condemning me and I stopped caring

what people think

But the one who was pointing the finger and condemning

was me.

So God forgave me, yet I hadn't forgave my self

And it was that day I literally felt, as the shame, guilt, and

unforgiveness left

So I'm free because God said so and no one else can

condemn me

Because He is all that matters, He is my everything.

Salvation Prayer

If you have ever found yourself struggling with sin and don't
know what to do,
If you find that you have fallen short, know God is there for
you.
God loves you so much that He sent His son to die for you
and me
If you are not saved, say this prayer because salvation is here
and free:
Lord I repent for all my sins, God I believe You sent Your
Son,
I believe Jesus died for my sins and rose in three days.
I believe in my heart and confess with my mouth
That Jesus Christ is Lord.
I thank You now Lord for Your gift of salvation and adopting
me as Your own
I'm ready to learn more about You and I know now I'm not
alone.
Guide me Lord and lead me as I seek to do Your will
Shake me, break me, mold me and all my old wounds heal.
Now as you read the word of God apply as much as you can
Know that God is all powerful and loving, He has the world
in the palm of His hands.

www.ingramcontent.com/pod-product-compliance
Lightning Source LLC
Chambersburg PA
CBHW060424050426
42449CB00009B/2118